The Old Woman who lived in a Shoe

Retold by
Russell Punter

Illustrated by Joelle Dreidemy

Reading Consultant: Alison Kelly
Roehampton University

There was an old
woman who lived
in a shoe.

She had so many children...

she didn't know
what to do.

There was Hannah
and Harry...

and Sara and Sam.

There was Aisha
and Abdul...

and Daisy and Dan.

There was Gwen
who was greedy...

and Stan who
was small.

There was Sean
who was short...

and Tom who was tall.

7

There was
Jasmine and Jeremy,
Sandeep and Grace...

boys and girls all
over the place.

Ying and Yasmin,
Jacob and Joe...

squeezed in together,
with no room to grow.

"This shoe is too full," said the woman, one day.

"We must get another.
I'll look right away."

With a list of the shoe stores...

she went to them all...

But the boots were too tiny...

and the shoes were too small.

She was on her
way home...

by the side of a river,

when she met
a huge giant.

He gave a sad shiver.

"Please help," sobbed the giant.

"There's a crab on my toe."

The old woman
took hold...

and pulled it off
– just like so.

"Thanks!" said the giant. "Now, can I help you?"

"Well," said the woman, "I would like your shoe."

"Of course," said the giant and he gave her his shoe.

"And for being so helpful, take the other one too."

Now all the children
have space to have fun.

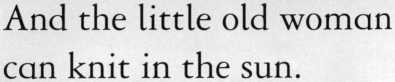

And the little old woman
can knit in the sun.

Puzzles

Puzzle 1

Can you spot the differences between these two pictures? There are six to find.

Puzzle 2
Find these things in the picture:

26

ball   old woman
birds   roof
chair   swing

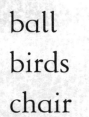

Puzzle 3

Put the pictures in order.

A

B

C

D

E

Puzzle 4
Find the opposites.

short

awake

asleep

happy

sad

tall

Answers to puzzles

Puzzle 1

Puzzle 2

roof   bird   bird

ball   old woman   chair   swing

Puzzle 3

C   A   E   B   D

Puzzle 4

short

tall

asleep

awake

sad

happy

About the story

The Old Woman Who Lived In A Shoe is based on an old nursery rhyme. It may have been written about Queen Caroline, the wife of King George II of England (1683-1760). The couple had eight children.

Series editor:
Lesley Sims

First published in 2008 by Usborne Publishing Ltd., Usborne House,
83-85 Saffron Hill, London EC1N 8RT, England. www.usborne.com
Copyright © 2008 Usborne Publishing Ltd.